The Greenhorn Gardening Guide

Keith O. Hankins

World rights reserved. This book or any portion thereof may not be copied or reproduced in any form or manner whatever, except as provided by law, without the written permission of the publisher, except by a reviewer who may quote brief passages in a review.

The author assumes full responsibility for the accuracy of all facts and quotations as cited in this book. The opinions expressed in this book are the author's personal views and interpretations, and do not necessarily reflect those of the publisher.

This book is provided with the understanding that the publisher is not engaged in giving spiritual, legal, medical, or other professional advice. If authoritative advice is needed, the reader should seek the counsel of a competent professional.

Copyright © 2018 Keith O. Hankins
Copyright © 2018 TEACH Services, Inc.
ISBN-13: 978-1-4796-0938-3 (Paperback)
Library of Congress Control Number: 2018948087

Contents

Introduction 5

So You Want To Start a Garden? 9

First Things First - Location 10

Size 14

Soil 18

Build 25

Plants and Planting 32

Maintain 43

Harvest 59

More To Learn 62

Plan Out Your Garden 64

Take Notes 68

Introduction

Gardening for me started when I was 14 years old. We were living in an apartment complex and the only soil we could call our own was a little 3'x3' square of dirt surrounded by fence and concrete. One day, I noticed my two younger siblings had thrown some rice into this little plot, their fingers frolicking in the soil. *What a waste,* I must've thought. *That's good food!* (Food was probably all I could think of as a growing boy.)

Time passed, and as I perchance peered around the red brick wall and glanced at the small patch of earth in the corner, I spotted emerald green blades of grass poking out of the soil. The rice had sprouted! *How intriguing! What else can we grow?* I wondered. *How about an avocado tree?* So we plopped a few of the tropical fruit's large, round, and brown seeds into our plant growth experimentation site and anticipated that we would soon have several avocado trees, their boughs bowing from the weight of innumerable buttery rich fruits.

Introduction

Alas, I forgot all about our avocado adventure (reason being, avocado seeds take two to six weeks just to germinate, not to mention that trees grown from seed usually take 3-15 *years* to bear fruit! Bummer right? I know. Anywho...) and moved on with life. Literally, we were moving on from our apartment and we had our sights set on someplace with more freedom than the dreary, concrete jungle we'd been living in for the past 3½ years.

Having all of our belongings packed and ready to go, I took a peek for the last time at our little plot of workable land. Lo and behold, the avocado seeds had sprouted and slender green stalks were shooting heavenward! *Wow! Let me dig some up so we can bring them with us!* In my excitement and awe at the biological miracle of plant growth, and the potential for myriads of avocados, I dug up a couple of the young plants in order to continue my horticultural escapade at our new destination. These later died (I never planted them for some reason), but I always wonder if maybe one of the remaining saplings grew into a bushy green avocado tree, bearing fruit for the next tenant of that apartment to enjoy. Looking back, I realize how much I could've actually grown in that small square of earth.

Fast-forward 2 years. I'm 16 and we're living in the country with one acre of land. This was obviously a huge upgrade and we had more land than we knew what to do with (from 9 square feet of earth to 40,000)!

I remember sitting down in our new country home and watching a documentary called *Back To Eden* starring Paul Gautschi and his beautiful, highly productive garden. After viewing this inspiring film, I was hooked. All I wanted to do was glean more information about gardening and learn how to be successful at it. That year I started a garden, with the help of my family, and we successfully produced tomatoes, okra, cucumbers, carrots, peppers, and more!

I had (and still have) so much fun producing something that people liked and that was actually beneficial to them. I've also learned so much from gardening and I believe that the experiences of overcoming difficulties, solving problems, obliterating tomato hornworms, and even failing at some crops have developed and strengthened the positive qualities and characteristics I have today.

Gardening will keep you active, broaden your knowledge about life in general, build character, strengthen your love/hate relationship with bugs,

Introduction

and provide you with your very own, homegrown, nutritious and flavor-filled food.

In the words of Gertrude Jekyll, *"The love of gardening is a seed once sown that never dies."* With this book I hope to sow that proverbial gardening seed, inspire you to try something new and exciting, and help you to put your heart and mind to an activity that is profitable for you in your sphere of influence.

So You Want To Start a Garden?

Here's what I want you to do: Go to Wal-Mart, Home-Depot, Lowes, or some other nursery or department store. Walk through the sliding door and buy yourself a nice sized gardening pot, a bag of compost, a tomato plant, some twine, and a good, sturdy stick. I promise that that little tomato plant will hand you a nice juicy tomato in due time! (Provided you water it and maybe flick off a couple of bugs.)

Although there may be more to gardening than what I've described above, playing in the dirt with seeds and veggies is fun and exciting, and it's also pretty hard to *completely* fail at it. The important thing is to just start! Precious time is wasted when one grovels in their fears and imaginary inadequacies. You can do it!

There are just a few things you might want to know in order for you to really be successful in this new adventure. Want to know what they are? (Go ahead and emphatically shout, "Yes!" Out loud please. LOUDER!) Great, let's get started!

First Things First – Location

Locating the spot for your garden is an important step, since this is where all of the miracles will happen. Here are a few things you need to consider when choosing a location for your garden.

Sunlight

Most garden plants need about six to eight hours of sunlight to grow their best. And to be specific, morning sunlight is much better than harsh afternoon heat. Try to situate your garden where it can get gentle light in the morning and dappled shade in the afternoon/evening.

In the Northern Hemisphere, your garden area should, ideally, be located on the southern side of your property to get the most sun (switch to the northern side for the Southern Hemisphere). Although the sun rises in the east and sets in the west, it doesn't go directly over your house in that direction. The diagram in Figure 1 will give you a general idea as to how the sun is positioned throughout the year.

As you can see, the sun actually passes over to the south of your house. Therefore, a garden that is situated on the south side of your property gets more sunlight than one situated on the northern side. Depending on your backyard layout, putting your garden on the south side of your property may or may not be feasible. However, regardless of where you position your garden or the positioning of the sun, the bottom line is that more exposure to the sun is better!

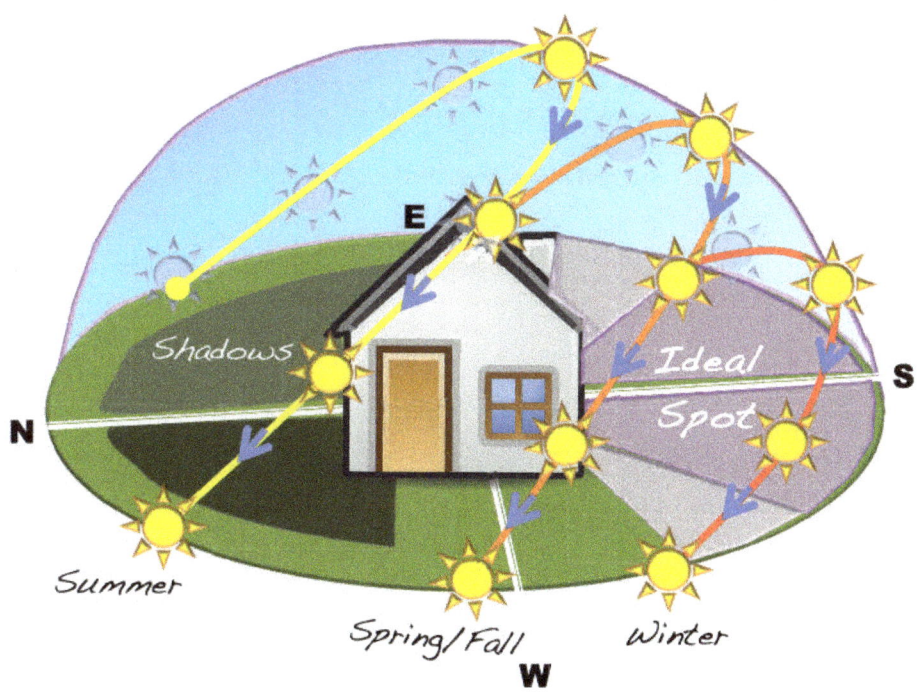

Figure 2

First Things First - Location

Water

Make sure that your garden is close to a water source, such as a garden hose or outdoor water faucet. A small garden doesn't need an extravagant water system to keep it healthy, so a watering can or an adjustable hose nozzle will do just fine.

Soil Safety

Before any planting begins, you will want to ensure that herbicides, pesticides, or any other harmful chemicals have not been recently used in the space where you plan to start your garden. These unfavorable substances will negatively affect the health of your plants and possibly the health of the consumers (by consumers, I mean you, your family, and anyone else with whom you may share your produce).

If you find that dangerous chemicals have been used in the desired planting area, you can either find another place to plant or shrug it off and hope for the best.

Wind

Adequate protection from strong winds can shelter young seedlings and transplants from stress, lessen the evaporation of water from the soil, and will cut back on soil erosion. Wind protection is only necessary if harsh winds are a significant, reoccurring problem.

Good View
Being able to see your garden through a window, or several windows, increases your chances of catching any problems before they get out of hand (e.g. pests, diseased leaves, your nosy neighbor). Having a good view of your garden will also make you think about and visit it more often. (Out of sight, out of mind.)

Accessibility
The absolute worst site to establish your garden would be in some out-of-the-way place, around a far corner, and too hard (at least it may seem too hard for some tired soul) to get to. Not only do you lack a *good view* of your garden, but your visits will also become less frequent, increasing the likelihood of other garden enthusiasts dropping by, such as pests, weeds, and disease.

Once you have determined the best site for your garden that has adequate sunlight, is close to a water source, has no harmful residues in the soil, is protected from harsh winds, and can easily be viewed and accessed, you will be ready to begin sizing your garden.

Size

Many new gardeners are so gung-ho about their new hobby that they're ready to plant everything they can think of in a supersized garden. They don't take into consideration the amount of time, work, and experience that is required to maintain such a large garden. Let me warn you now, gardening takes time and effort.

> *It's one thing to drop a seed or plant into the ground; it's another thing to be able to keep it alive (and help it to thrive) until harvest time.*

The Greenhorn Gardening Guide

This is why you're going to start *small*. Starting small means that your first garden will be more like an incentive to do it again next year. You can also consider it as a test garden to discover what works for you, what plants you like best, how your climate and weather patterns affect your gardening, and so on.

However, this doesn't mean that you won't get a bountiful harvest from your small, experimental garden! There are many ways to grow a lot of food in a little space.

Square Foot

One such way to get the most out of your garden plot is by using the "Square Foot Gardening" method, popularized by Mel Bartholomew. It's not only simple to set up, but it helps you to estimate how much you can plant in the space you have. Here's how it works:

Think In Squares

This method is called "Square Foot" because that's the way everything is simply, yet precisely, laid out. Everything is based on square feet.

To start off, let's use a simple 4'x4' square (or 16 square feet). This may not seem like a lot of space

Size

to garden in, but, believe it or not, Figure 2 shows all that you can grow in a plot this small.

1 Head of Cabbage	1 Head of Broccoli	4 Heads of Romaine Lettuce	4 Heads of Redina Lettuce
4 Bunches of Spinach	4 Bunches of Swiss Chard	4 Stalks of Corn	9 Onions
1 Tomato Plant	1 Pepper Plant	1 Eggplant Plant	1 Potato Plant
9 Red Beets	9 Golden Beets	16 Carrots	16 Radishes

4'x4'

Figure 2

All of this food growing in a space smaller than a dining table? That's pretty amazing!

Now, just one of these plots may be a little too small for the amount of food you want to grow. If that is the case, two to four of these 4x4 foot squares should be the perfect amount to kick off your gardening experience.

We'll discuss more about the "Square Foot Gardening" method in this guide, but first we need to take a look at the *most important* feature of your garden. It is literally the foundation on which everything grows, and if it isn't just right, then you'll have some problems on your hands. What am I talking about? Soil!

Greenhorn Guidance: If you like the idea of square foot gardening, check out the **All New Square Foot Gardening** book by Mel Bartholomew to learn more in-depth what this method is all about.

Soil

> "When the soil is deficient,
> the plants also are deficient and weakened,
> and they lose their defenses."
> – Charlotte Gerson

I would add that when the plants are deficient, the human body, which is consuming that plant, would also be deficient in the vitamins and minerals that its food is lacking. This is one of the main causes of disease in the world — the lack of proper nutrients in our food.

Obviously, soil is very important to the health of the plants growing in it. For this reason, I don't recommend planting in just any type of soil. In order to provide the most ideal environment for your veggies, you should create your own soil mix on top of the existing ground in your garden area.

Ingredients for *Ideal* Soil

You will need (by volume) approximately:
- ⅓ Compost
  (Best if from 3-5 different sources to get a wider range of nutrients)

- ⅓ Peat Moss
  (let expand once removed from bag to get proper portions)
- ⅓ Vermiculite

Mel Bartholomew, the author of *Square Foot Gardening*, has coined this soil combination as *Mel's Mix*. He claims that with this medley of organic materials you'll *never* need to fertilize, because all of the nutrients and trace minerals that your plants need will be contained in the different compost sources you use.

To determine how much of this mixture you'll need for a given space, simply multiply the dimensions of that space. For example, if you were to fill up a box that was 3'x2'x1' with this mixture, then you would multiply these dimensions to get the box's volume of six cubic feet. Then you could fill the box with ⅓, or two cubic feet, of each ingredient.

These three parts of your soil blend should be mixed up evenly in order to guarantee that everybody growing in your garden gets an equal share of the goodness. Now, Let's explore the benefits of each of these soil components.

Soil

Compost
- It adds great soil structure.
- It is filled with beneficial microorganisms.
- It is rich with nutrients.

Peat Moss
- It manages water very efficiently.
- It holds on to some nutrients that leach out of the soil.
- One application of peat moss will last for several years.

Vermiculite
- It helps keep soil light.
- It allows for good airflow.
- It absorbs and retains water.

Greenhorn Guidance: All of the materials I mention in this book can easily be found at a local nursery, large department store, or online. If for any reason you're not able to acquire these materials, then just start with what you have. Can't buy peat moss or vermiculite? Research alternatives or just try gardening without them. I don't want you to be discouraged from starting because of a lack of resources or funds.

The Greenhorn *Gardening* Guide

When I first started gardening, not only was I oblivious to what vermiculite and peat moss were, I didn't even know they existed. All I knew to grow in was the earth I stood on, cow manure from over the barbed wire fence, and later donkey manure from just about everywhere on our one acre property. (Yes we had a donkey, and no he wasn't potty trained.) With those resources and some free hardwood tree mulch, I produced my own food, and quite a bit of it. Did I mention that all of these resources were free (including the donkey)? I grew more fresh produce while gardening with unconventional resources and limited knowledge, than not gardening at all.

Remember, all you really need to get started is a plant (or seeds), soil, water, and light (You don't even need sunlight in some cases). Make the best with what you have, learn from difficulties or mistakes, and have fun!

Contact or visit your local Cooperative Extension Service to learn more about soil and to get a soil test. Soil tests measure the nutrient levels of your soil, which will help you find out whether your soil may be missing vital ingredients for plant health. In some states you can get a free soil test through

Soil

your Cooperative Extension Service, and they can also help analyze the information for you.

If you find out, through a soil test or clues given from your plants, that your soil is missing some nutrients, then you may need to add some additional materials. For example, soft rock phosphate works well for soil lacking in phosphorus, limestone is great for soil that is too acidic, and nitrogen helps for plants to grow green and strong.

The pH of Soil

Just a moment ago, I mentioned that limestone helps to correct soil that is too acidic. The acidity or alkalinity of your soil is measured by the pH scale and determines how well your veggie's roots can absorb nutrients from the earth. Figure 3 illustrates a basic pH scale.

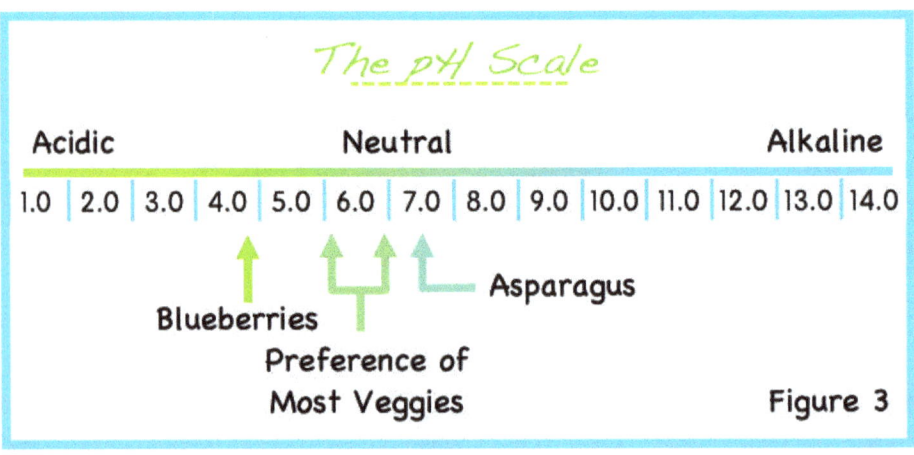

Most garden plants like a neutral pH level — not too acidic, not too alkaline — in order for them to most effectively mine nutrients from the soil. (Neutral on the pH scale would be denoted by the value 7.0 while smaller values are more acidic and larger values are more alkaline.) Exceptions would be plants like blueberries, cranberries, and potatoes, which like a more acidic soil.

There are a couple of ways to change your soil pH if for some reason it's tipping the scale too far either way. For example, if you wanted a more acidic soil pH, then you could add sulfur or peat moss to raise the levels a bit.

If excessive alkalinity is an issue, then limestone or wood ash amendments will effectively tip the pH scale in your veggie's favor. Compost, mulch, and other organic materials tend to even out and neutralize soil levels.

With the soil we've created you shouldn't have any problems with your pH or nutrient levels. You may not even need to fertilize if you use several types of compost, which assures a wide range of essential nutrients and minerals.

Soil

But before you construct this soil mix, you need some place to put it and not just in any place. You need something that will contain it, keep your garden clean and decorative, and help organize how you plant so that you can be completely efficient with every seed and transplant. For this, you're going to have to build!

Build

Straw bale gardening, lasagna gardening, container gardening hugelkultur, Back to Eden, permaculture, agriscaping, hydroponics, aquaponics, and, old-fashioned, traditional gardening. There are dozens of ways to build a garden and everyone has their own preference.

You should research these and other methods to see which type works best for you and your situation. In this book, though, we'll be adapting our garden techniques from the "Square Foot Gardening" method as mentioned before in the "Size" chapter. Square foot gardening is simple, and its principles can be applied to most other types of gardening.

Let's recap what we've learned about "Square Foot Gardening". We want everything based on square feet, and our ideal sized plot is 16 square feet. Also, to start off with, you may want two to four plots of this size.

The easiest, cleanest, and most productive way to do this is to make two to four wooden garden boxes, that are four feet long, and four feet wide.

Build

These boxes should also be at least 6 inches deep, but 8-12 inches would be even better. You need enough rich, loose soil in order to grow a number of different varieties of plants that have different root lengths. You don't want long-type carrots bending every which way because there isn't an adequate amount of soil.

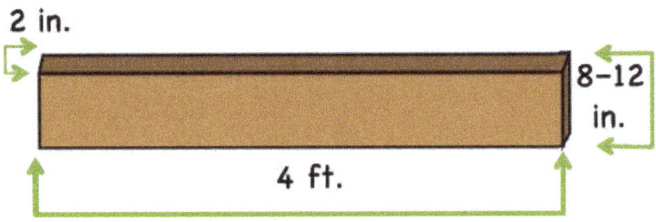

What You'll Need (per box)
- Four (2in. x 8-12in. x 4ft.) Wood Boards
- 12 Screws

That's it! All you need for these easy garden boxes are four pieces of wood and three screws per corner. Figure 4 shows what the finished product should look like.

Figure 4

The Greenhorn Gardening Guide

Now to make this even cleaner and more organized you're going to put a grid on top of the box (after you fill it with soil). There are two ways to do this. You can use some type of sturdy string (like fishing line), or you can use wooden laths, which is more artistic and will last longer.

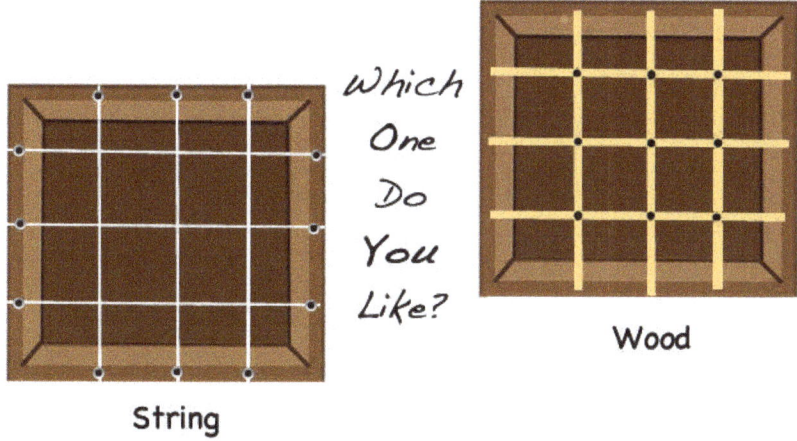

String

Wood

Line Grid

To make the line grid you'll need (per box):
- 12 half inch screws
- 25 feet of string

Instructions:
- Starting 12 inches in, drill screws ¾ way down into wood at 12-inch intervals around the perimeter of the box.
- Tie the string onto adjacent screws as shown in the illustration.

Build

Pros: Cost efficient; Fairly easy to set up.
Cons: May eventually break; May be hard to see grid lines; Not removable.

Wooden Lath Grid

To make the wooden lath grid you'll need (per box):
- Six (1/4" x 1.5" x 4') Wooden Laths used for Lattices
- 9 half-inch screws

Instructions:
- Line three laths parallel of each other 12 inches apart.
- Lay the other three laths perpendicular to and on top of the first three at 12 inches apart.
- Drill screws in at the 9 cross sections.

Pros: Decorative; Sturdy; Easier to see; Removable.
Cons: May cost a little more (not much); May rot if not protected.

Now, if you prefer not to build anything and just have a woodless raised bed, that will work too, but there are some drawbacks to doing it that way. Your soil will wash away much easier without the barrier, and weeds or invasive grasses will enjoy slowly crawling into your open bed.

Not to mention you'll miss out on the handsome, aesthetic look of a rustic, golden-brown box filled with your favorite fresh fruits and veggies!

If you really want this gardening setup, but don't have the time to do it, check out these online stores for a quick (but expensive) solution:
- SquareFootGardening.com
- GardenInMinutes.com/shop

Grass and Weeds

After you place your newly made boxes in the most ideal location, you need to lay some type of material at the bottom of the box to keep grass and weeds from growing from below. Here are a couple of things you can use for your weed barrier:

Newspaper will do just fine
Best Price: Free
- Try to find free, non-glossed newspaper and lay down several layers of it to kill grass before it decomposes.
- Make sure to overlap pages and stick some under the edge of the box to keep grass or weeds from sneaking into it.

Build

Cardboard is even better
Best Price: Free
- Old cardboard boxes work in the same way newspaper does, but you don't need nearly as many layers.
- Make sure to overlap and have some sticking under the edges.

Biodegradable Weed Barrier for long-lasting, sure-fire control
Best Price: $10±
- Apply only one layer in the same way as cardboard and newspaper (Or follow instructions on packaging).

Adding Soil
Now you can fill your boxes with soil. To do so, grab all of the ingredients to your soil (peat moss, vermiculite, and compost) and pour the proper parts

into your garden box. Then you can mix it evenly together with a shovel, pitchfork, or any other tool of your choice.

Alright! Now that you have your newly created boxes filled with some nutrient rich soil (or your garden bed prepared in whatever method or style you have chosen), it's time to move onto the next step and put something inside of these garden beds to get things growing!

Plants and Planting

This is obviously one of the most important parts of the gardening process because without it you'd have no food! Here are some things you need to think about to have successful plants.

What To Plant

Finding out what to plant is based entirely on what you WANT to plant. Many people find that they plant different types of vegetables that they don't even like to eat!

To make sure that this isn't you, write down a list of all of your favorite vegetables, greens, beans, and fruits so you can have a visual of what you actually like.

Another factor in deciding what to plant is what time of the year it is. Whether it's spring, summer, fall, or winter, there's always something you can plant; you just have to make sure it's the right plant for the right season.

Keep in mind that climate and weather behavior will change and varies greatly from state to state. While one may be able to grow tomatoes through

November in the South (without cold protection), folks more north may have started their winter crops back in August!

Figure 5 shows a table of some plants that grow best in each season.

SPRING	SUMMER	FALL	WINTER
POTATOES	TOMATOES	BROCCOLI	ONIONS
LETTUCE	SWEET POTATOES	KOHLRABI	BOK CHOY
CARROTS	CUCUMBER	LEEKS	CABBAGE
COLLARDS	MELONS	SPINACH	GARLIC
ENGLISH PEAS	PEPPERS	BEETS	KALE

Figure 5

How Much To Plant

Deciding how much you want to or can plant is determined by how much space you have and how big your chosen plants grow. Since all plants need a little (or a lot of) space to grow, you'll know how much space they need by how big they are when they're mature.

Plants And Planting

For example, a head of lettuce may be 8-inches wide when it's fully grown. Therefore, when you sow seeds or plant a transplant, you know that each plant needs about 8 inches of space. Now you know how much you can plant with the space that you have. Also, don't forget about *air* space. There are dozens of ideas on how to build your garden upwards (through trellises, terraces, hanging baskets and pots, etc.) to take advantage of *all* of the space you may have available to you. Search *"space saving gardening ideas"* on the web and you just might find something that you like, is cost efficient (maybe even free), and effective.

Sometimes you decide how much to plant by planting more than you actually need. This way, you can be sure that you get the amount of produce you want in spite of pest, disease, or weather damage.

When To Plant

It is best to transplant plants in the early morning, in the evening, or on an overcast day so that plants can have some time to adjust to their new setting without harsh sunlight beating down on them. Be sure to water plants deeply after planting in order to decrease plant stress even more.

Sow seeds on a calm day with no heavy rain in the forecast, which can wash seeds and seedlings away.

The Greenhorn Gardening Guide

Water seeds lightly both after sowing and when the soil begins to dry, to ensure they germinate in a timely manner. (If the soil dries out for too long, then seeds will take longer than usual to germinate.)

How To Plant

Knowing how to properly plant or sow seeds determines whether or not your young transplants or seedlings will grow into vibrant, healthy plants.

Transplants

Buying vegetable transplants from a nursery or department store is the easiest way to start planting right away. All you have to do is pick your favorite plants, make sure they are healthy and have no pests on them, and bring them home to place in your garden. Instructions on the plant's tag will help guide you when planting.

Sowing

Sowing seeds is a little more challenging than planting transplants, but it is a lot cheaper. Some seeds are large and easy to sow; others are very tiny and require a little patience to grow successfully.

It's good practice to sow seeds in little pots or seed trays way before you need them so that you can transplant them outside as early as possible. You

Plants And Planting

can also do this to have extra plants to replace the ones that you eat up from the garden.

Starting out, it's best to buy transplants for plants like tomatoes, peppers, and celery because these need a lot of care when planting from seed. Lettuce, radish, and corn are a few examples of plants that can easily be planted by seed. Most seed packets will tell you at what depth to sow seeds, how many seeds to sow in one spot, how far to space seeds, how far to thin seedlings, and days till harvest.

Spacing

Since you're planting by square feet, you usually space a plant according to what a plant tag or seed package advises. The information on a plant's tag or seed packet will tell you what the maturity size is (how big it will be when it's ready to produce fruit, be eaten, or cease growing) or how far to space your plants.

The back of a seed packet will generally have three suggestions for how far to space your seeds. The first one tells you how far apart to space rows. We won't follow this suggestion because we aren't planting with the traditional row method. We're planting in boxes that can easily be reached into and that don't need space for tractor wheels or foot traffic.

The second suggestion tells you how far apart to sow seeds in a row. It doesn't make sense to plant at these spacings either because one: these spacings are much too close together, and two: the seed packets tell us to do something funny in the third spacing suggestion when we sow seeds this close.

The third suggestion tells you how far to "thin" seedlings. Thinning is when you pull out some seedlings to make more space for the others, but why sow seeds to just pull them out a little while later? Not only is that a waste of time, but a waste of money! Instead, we will completely ignore the first two spacing suggestions on a seed packet and sow seeds at the thinning distance. This allows enough space for the plants to grow to their full size and no space for weeds to grow with them.

For example, if a package says to sow seeds 3 inches apart and then thin to 6 inches, sow seeds instead at 6 inches to save both seeds and time.

Figure 6 shows a piece of one of your 16 square foot boxes. Square Foot #1 shows an example of 8 – 12-inch spacing. If a plant needs 8 – 12 inches of space, it takes one square foot all by itself (unless you can fit some smaller plants around it).

Plants And Planting

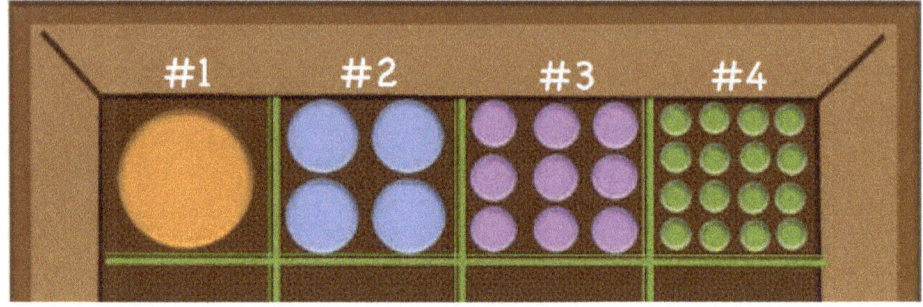

Figure 6

Square Foot #2 shows 6-inch spacing. With this amount of space, you can fit four plants in one square foot. Square Foot #3 shows 4-inch spacing and Square Foot #4 shows 3-inch spacing. You can fit 9 plants and 16 plants, respectively, in each square foot, with the suggested spacing.

If certain types of plants need 18 inches of space or more, you should plant them in every other square to give them the space they need.

Placement

When you sow seeds or plant transplants, you always want to make sure that one plant will not block sunlight from another. Just like your house or trees can shade your garden, tall plants can shade small plants.

To avoid this problem, put taller plants on the north side of your garden and smaller plants on the south side. Remember the sunlight diagram from the

The Greenhorn Gardening Guide

Location section? When the sun comes up, all of the shade will be cast towards the north. If your plants rise in height from south to north, than all will receive proper lighting.

The only exception to this would be when a plant like lettuce needs to be shaded from the sun in the heat of summer. When you have that situation just interplant the lettuce with a larger plant like tomatoes.

Plants And Planting

Succession Planting

If you want to continually harvest produce throughout the season, you may want to try succession planting. When you succession plant, only plant part of your first crop and then wait a few weeks before planting another part or the remainder of that same crop. In this way you will stagger and lengthen your harvesting times. Figure 7 illustrates how succession planting would work in part of your gardening box.

As shown in the illustration, "CIRCLE" has been planted in the first square foot in Week 1 and two weeks were allowed before we planted another CIRCLE. The full crop of CIRCLE is planted four times in this way to fill up the space designated for it. In this example, CIRCLE will be ready to harvest in six weeks, the second planting of CIRCLE will be ready two weeks after that, and the same will be true for planting three and four.

Let's say that one planting of CIRCLE can be harvested for only 1 week and then it dies or stops producing (although most real plants will produce much longer than 1 week). Let's also imagine that one planting of CIRCLE will last you 2 weeks in the fridge (much longer in the freezer).

The Greenhorn Gardening Guide

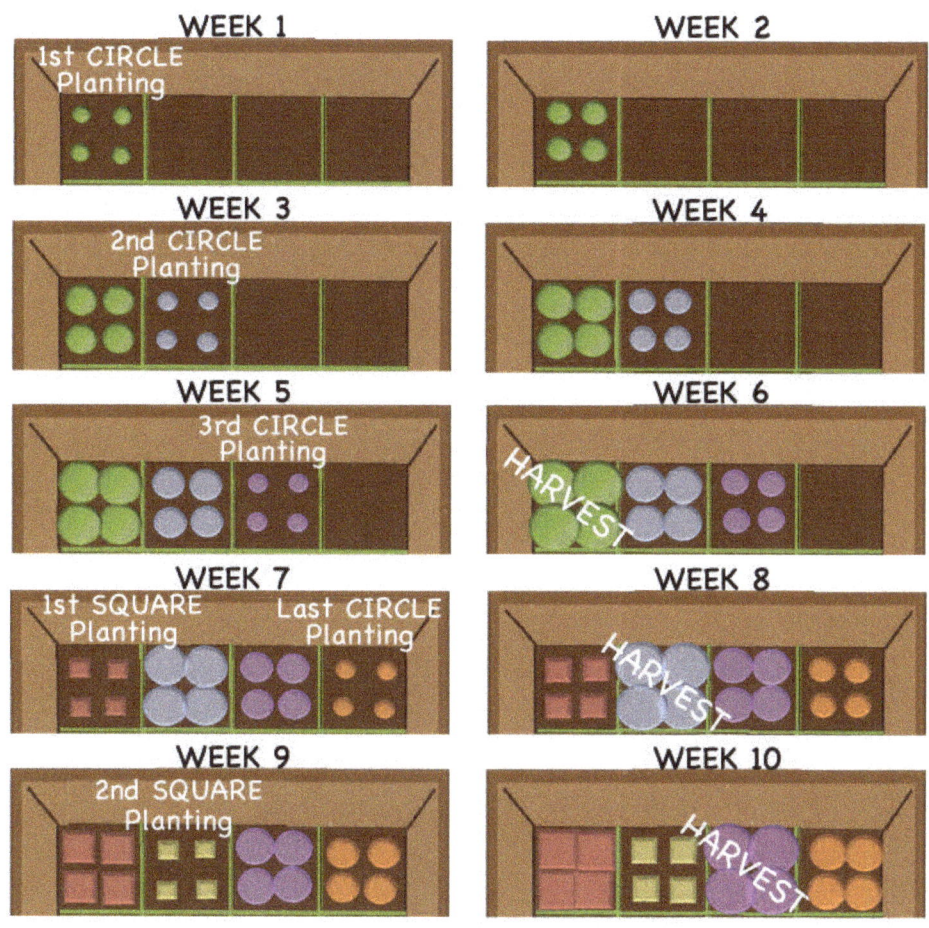

Figure 7

With succession planting, you'll be harvesting and eating fresh CIRCLE for nearly 2 months and you only planted in a fourth of your box! Not to mention SQUARE, which is steadily growing where your first plantings of CIRCLE used to be (Yum... CIRCLE and SQUARE). This goes to show that a little patience really does go a long way!

Plants And Planting

We've just discussed what is probably the second most exciting part of growing your own food, but gardening doesn't stop with *planting* your favorite fruits and veggies (and maybe flowers). You'll need to *take care* of your garden with due diligence to keep your plants healthy and happy until harvest time.

Maintain

> "A garden requires patient labor and attention. Plants do not grow merely to satisfy ambitions or to fulfill good intentions. They thrive because someone expended effort on them."
> – Gertrude Jekyll

For many people, the hardest part of gardening is maintenance. But it doesn't have to be. Taking care of the garden will be fun and less than a workout when using this method of gardening. Other methods, such as lasagna gardening and container gardening, are also less intensive than most methods and are great for youngsters as well as those who may be past their prime.

Hydroponic and aquaponics methods don't require much work at all after the initial setup, but all methods require diligence and must be maintained properly to help plants make it to the finish line. Here are the top four things to focus on to keep your garden thriving until harvest time.

Maintain

1. Water

What's too much? What's too little? When should you do it? What's the best way to do it? How often should you do it? Why are there so many questions?

Let's answer the last question first. Water is very important to your garden. A well-watered garden will flourish and produce juicy, luscious produce, but a garden watered the wrong way can cause disease, pests, and dry, withered plants that may never make it to harvest time.

Too Much Water

You know you've watered too much when you can squeeze water out of your soil. When soil is waterlogged it suffocates roots and causes them to rot, which means the death of your plants.

The main symptom of a plant in waterlogged soil is wilted leaves. This is also a sign of other serious diseases so make sure to check that soggy soil is actually the problem.

Too Little Water

When the top inch of your soil is dry, you need to water. If more than an inch of soil is dry, then your plants may begin to suffer from water stress. Lack of water will also wilt the leaves on your plants or they may curl up to reduce water evaporation.

When To Water

The best time to water is in the morning. This gives roots time to absorb the water, and it helps the plants survive the heat of the day.

The second best time to water your garden is in the evening. Your plants will have a lot more time to absorb the water this way without any sun, but you need to make sure that plant leaves have time to dry off before nightfall. Cool, damp leaves provide an enticing environment for disease.

Best Way To Water

When you water some of your plants, especially seedlings, you want to mimic light rainfall. This way, all the soil is evenly watered, seedlings don't get dislodged from the soil, and soil is not washed away.

On other plants, like tomatoes and peppers, it's best to water at the base of the plant to avoid getting the leaves wet. Some plants are susceptible to diseases from bacteria and fungi that splash up from the soil. Watering carefully from below the leaves will minimize this risk.

In a small garden it's doesn't take much time to carefully water your garden, but if time is limited, or if you won't be home for a while, than you may want to install a simple irrigation system.

Maintain

Greenhorn Guidance: Here's a quick, easy, and cheap way to irrigate your plants without having to stand around with a watering can. Take an old hose and measure out how much you'd need to line your garden area and to reach from the closest water faucet to your garden. Poke holes in the hose at 3"-6" apart with a screwdriver, drill, or other tool starting where the hose reaches the garden soil. Make sure the holes are facing down.

Cut the rest of the hose away a couple feet after your last hole. Bend the end of the hose and secure it to create pressure inside of your irrigation system. Once this is set up, all you have to do is turn the faucet on enough for there to be a trickle of water which will irrigate your plants without getting any leaves wet or causing a muddy mess (as long as you remember to turn it off)!

2. Fertilizer

As I mentioned in the "Soil" chapter of this book, it is claimed that with ideal soil or *Mel's Mix,* created by Mel Bartholomew, you'll never need to fertilize. Reason being, all of the nutrients and minerals needed for growth are already present because of all of the different types of compost you used.

The Greenhorn Gardening Guide

It doesn't hurt to give your plants an extra boost though if you see that they're not growing or performing as you think they should, especially if you decide not to use the ideal soil mixture I described and plant straight in the ground. Here's a quick rundown on fertilizer.

Scientists today report that at least 16 nutrients are needed for plants to grow. Most fertilizer's focus on the three most important, which are Nitrogen, Phosphorus, and Potassium (abbreviated by their chemical symbols, NPK, on fertilizer containers). Plants can easily obtain the next three, carbon, hydrogen, and oxygen, from their environment. The remaining 10 secondary and micronutrients are received from the soil that plants grow in.

If the soil doesn't contain these vital nutrients and minerals, then, as a quick fix, you'll need to apply fertilizer. There are two generally recognized methodologies to fertilizer, but I would like to present three.

Conventional

This first methodology uses the synthetic chemical forms of substances that plants need to grow. Conventional fertilizers are water-soluble (they dissolve in water) and can be absorbed by plant

Maintain

roots quickly. For this reason, they became a favorite tool among farmers and gardeners alike in the early 20th century to speedily increase crop yields and performance.

While chemical fertilizers were indeed a boon to the productivity of these farmers, it was also one of the reasons why modern agricultural farms stopped practicing traditional soil fertility methods (such as composting and crop rotation). As a result, the southern plains of the U.S. suffered one of the greatest environmental disasters caused by man, the Dust Bowl. They didn't *maintain* their gardens.

Fertilizer ratios measure the nutrients readily available for plant consumption and represent the percentage of each nutrient contained in a particular product. Since conventional fertilizers specialize in quick absorption, their NPK levels will have high values such as 10-10-10 or 20-20-20. Nitrogen, Phosphorus, and Potassium (N-P-K) correspond with each number respectively.

Organic
This second fertilization methodology, which spans over much more than just the subject of fertilizer, concerns producers as well as consumers. Organic practices were the norm until we decided chemicals synthesis was better at producing food than nature

was. For several decades now, health and environmentally conscientious people have advocated organic food, mainly combating GMOs, chemical sprays, and artificially nourished vegetables.

Organic gardening is basically an imitation of how plant ecology works in nature, which includes the death of plants and animals, their reincorporation into the soil, and the natural production of fertilizer from the decomposition of that plant and animal matter.

Gardeners imitate this process by composting plant waste and applying it to their gardens, which encourages earthworms and microbes to live in the soil. Conversely, conventional fertilizer, in excess, has an inhospitable, acidifying affect on soils, which tends to repel worms from dutifully restoring the soil.

Other plant and animal byproducts, such as seaweed, cotton, wood ashes, manure, bones, and even blood, are used as organic fertilizers and are applied only when soil tests or plants show signs of nutrient deficiency. Sustainability and conservation are also important, and regulate the use of certain non-renewable sources such as rock-based fertilizers and other mined substances.

Maintain

Organic fertilizers release nutrients into the soil slower than conventional fertilizers do and will have lower N-P-K levels such as 5-3-3 (fish meal) or 3-11-0 (bone meal). Many organic fertilizers specialize in one nutrient, resulting in a NPK level that looks something like 0-3-0 (rock phosphate) or 13-0-0 (feather meal).

Fertilizers with higher ratios will most likely have synthetic chemicals in them and aren't organic. Look for fertilizers that have the OMRI (Organic Materials Review Institute) seal because these are certified organic.

Veganic

Largely an unknown ideology, various veganic methods have been propagated (no pun intended) throughout the 1900s and many people are unknowingly following its principles. The term comes from the blending of *vegetarian* and *organic*.

Much like organic agriculture, "Veganicism" (I don't think this is a word) focuses on natural fertilization, sustainability, and rejects chemical sprays. But veganic fertilization has one more caveat. Unlike organic gardening, animal-based fertilizers such as bone meal, blood meal, and fish emulsion, are rejected for these reasons: antibiotics, hormones, chemicals, disease, and pests.

Farm animals are regularly injected with antibiotics and hormones to enhance their growth and productivity. Pesticides and herbicides, sprayed onto livestock crops, also end up into their feed. All of these harmful substances are found in their fertilizer byproducts.

Bovine Spongiform Encephalopathy, aka Mad Cow Disease, which has a possible link to the Creutzfeldt-Jakob disease, may infect humans through bone meal fertilizers. E. coli and parasites, found in animal intestines, also show up in manures used for agricultural use. These are avoided with veganic gardening.

Claims have been made that veganic fertilization methods have resulted in decreased pest problems compared to organic and conventional practices.

Veganic fertilizers will be mostly plant or rock derived. These have low NPK levels such as 1-0.5-2.5 (kelp) or 0-0-7 (green sand).

Although I have presented this information with a hint of bias, I hope it adequately introduced you to

Maintain

the world of fertilizer and helps you to make an informed decision on fertilizing methods.

But don't stop with just this information! Continue to do your own research so that you know for yourself the reason behind your gardening practices. In the end, the choice is yours, but so are the consequences.

3. Weeds

With the soil mix that you'll be using, weeds will be a breeze! Literally. The only weeds that get into your garden will be the ones blown in by the wind. These are super easy to get rid of, though, because your soil will be loose and the young weeds won't have enough time to send out their nutrient-sapping roots before you effortlessly slip them from out of the soil.

If you want extra protection against weeds, then just apply some mulch! Mulch can consist of wood chips, leaves, straw, or any other organic matter that will prevent weed seeds from entering your soil or emerging from it.

Greenhorn Guidance: There is a difference between straw and hay. Straw is usually harvested before it produces seeds while hay will *most likely* contain grass seeds within it. In light of this, avoid using hay as mulch; introducing grass seeds to your garden would be counter-productive.) There are other types of mulch you may want to avoid also so do your research before applying.

---

4. Pests

The dreaded word. There are many types and species of bugs and beetles, worms and caterpillars, rodents and birds, that just love to destroy our crops (too many to talk about here). But, there are also many beneficial bugs and animals that love to eat those other pests.

You'll want to be able to identify both good and bad critters, so take a look at Figure 8, which shows a few examples of beneficial and destructive bugs, just to get you started. Identify these animals and many more so you can know how to handle and identify problems better.

Make sure to look up the creepy-crawlies that you're not sure about and see whether they're beneficial or harmful. This is important because, often, one bug can devour an entire plant. Some bugs even transmit diseases to your plant when feeding on it, which can be equally devastating, as well.

Maintain

Figure 8

Getting Rid Of Pests

There are several organic ways to get rid of pests. The number one best way is to keep your plants healthy! A healthy plant can take care of pests and disease all by itself.

Nevertheless, plants won't be able to *stay* healthy without pest removal. The easiest (organic) methods are to manually pick them off of your plants or dunk them in soapy water.

Soap causes the cell membranes of an insect to break and it can also remove the protective cover of an insect, causing death through excess loss of water.

Squirt and stir some soap into a bucket of water and drop bugs that you catch into it. You can also put about a teaspoon of pure Castile or organic insecticidal soap (dish soap works too, but never laundry detergent) into a large spray bottle to spray insects directly.

Be sure to test the spray on a leaf first to make sure that it doesn't burn foliage after a couple of hours. Furthermore, keep in mind that soap will also kill beneficial insects like ladybugs and spiders (yes spiders are beneficial, so leave them be unless

Maintain

they're venomous), so be careful to only spray the bad guys.

There are also commercial pesticides that are classified as organic, but should only be used as a last resort as they can still be harmful to humans and animal life, if abused. Always research the most efficient and effective way to deal with a particular pest.

Remember, the best weapon to keep your garden safe from plant-destroying pests is to spend time in your garden. A lot is seen this way.

Disease

The other dreaded word. Diseases are just as devastating to the garden as pests are, maybe worse depending on your region and environment. This doesn't mean they can't be beat, though. You can avoid a lot of disease damage by following these three very important principles:

1. Keep Plants Healthy

A plant isn't unhealthy because it is diseased; it is diseased because it's unhealthy. A plant kept healthy, by providing it nutrient-filled soil, adequate water, clean air, and sufficient sunlight, will be able to handle disease better.

2. Prevention

> *"An ounce of prevention is worth a pound of cure."*
> – Benjamin Franklin

You can prevent disease by blocking the avenues through which it enters. Soil-borne bacteria, plant wounds, pests, and other pathways for disease are easier to fix then a diseased plant.

- Cover soil with mulch so that bacteria or fungi can't splash onto leaves when there's rain or when you're watering.

- Be tender when dealing with your plants to avoid causing wounds on them.

- Eradicate or protect plants against pests before they can cause damage to plants, making them more susceptible to disease.

3. Purging

If one of your plants is infected with a disease with no hope of recovery, it is best to remove it from the garden and trash it. Holding on to the plant will give the disease a chance to spread to your

Maintain

other plants, causing them all to be lost. Don't let one "bad apple" spoil the whole bunch!

If you can keep your plants healthy and safe from pests, diseases, and bad weather for the duration of their growing period, you'll be able to reap the fruits (and vegetables) of your labor before you can say, "Harvest!"

Harvest

It's finally time to pull, pluck, and pick your own, homegrown, sweet, succulent, and chemical-free food! It's the best part of the gardening experience!

You'll need to research the best way to harvest the produce from the specific plants you choose. Some you should handpick, others you should cut cleanly with a sharp blade, and some you should just pull up the whole thing!

Whichever method you have to use, make sure to use it quickly. Some produce gets bitter, squishy, or woody if left alone too long. You could also find that something else decided to harvest for you, like a squirrel or rabbit.

In order to harvest at the right time check the date you planted and how long the plants take to mature. Mark these things down on a calendar for a visual reminder. This way you'll be ready to harvest when the time comes.

Sometimes you can tell if something is ready to harvest just by looking at it, like tomatoes, peppers, or strawberries. You still want to mark maturity

Harvest

dates down so you can be ready for the abundance of fresh produce!

After the growing period for a crop is finished and you've harvested all you can, pull up the remains of the plant and add compost to the area to replenish the nutrients that have been used. (You don't need to add any more peat moss or vermiculite because these will last in the soil for several years.) After this, you can plant another of your favorite fruit or vegetable and prepare for another harvest!

Greenhorn Guidance: Make sure to be cautious when eating your produce if you've used manure, pesticides (even organic), fungicides, or herbicides (not recommended) in your garden. If you have used these substances, it is best to wash your fruits and veggies thoroughly to avoid E. coli, salmonella, or chemical poisoning. Even if you haven't used these substances, washing your hands and food before consumption is still good hygienic practice!

So when you're out in the garden and you see a big, juicy, crimson-red tomato, glistening in the early morning sunlight, weigh the consequences of plucking

The Greenhorn Gardening Guide

it right off the vine, ignoring the warning above, and impulsively sinking your teeth into your very own, homegrown, nutritious and flavor-filled food!

More To Learn

Now that you have read through this guide and understand some of the basics of gardening, you can go and research anything and everything else you need to know. There are so many resources and people to learn and gather information from that you'll soon know more than you ever thought you would about what you typically bring home from the grocery store.

Research is key to successful gardening and it's fun, too! Below, I've provided a few resources that have benefited me in my own gardening adventures.

Remember, have fun, be diligent, and share with others what you learn and harvest. Happy greenhorn gardening!

Recommended Reading

There are thousands of books on the subject of gardening, each one having it's own style and methods. Here are a few books that have helped me in my gardening.

All New Square Foot Gardening

Mel Bartholomew

Rodale's Vegetable Garden Problem Solver

Fern Marshall Bradley

Rodale's Ultimate Encyclopedia of Organic Gardening
Fern Marshall Bradley, Barbara W. Ellis, Ellen Phillips
Small-Plot, High-Yield Gardening
Sal Gilbertie & Larry Sheehan
What's Wrong With My Vegetable Garden?
David Deardorff & Kathryn Wadsworth
The New Victory Garden
Bob Thompson

Recommended Websites

There are loads of gardening websites, blogs, and YouTube channels that have loads of information on how to garden. Dig the web for tons of exciting information from sites like these:

Almanac.com/Gardening
BHG.com/Gardening
BonniePlants.com
BurpeeHomeGardens.com/GardenHelp
EpicGardening.com
GardeningKnowHow.com
HomeGuides.sfgate.com/Garden
MotherEarthNews.com/Organic-Gardening
SquareFootGardening.com
WikiHow.com

Plan Out Your Garden

What do you want to grow? Where do you want to grow it? Draw out your plans here!

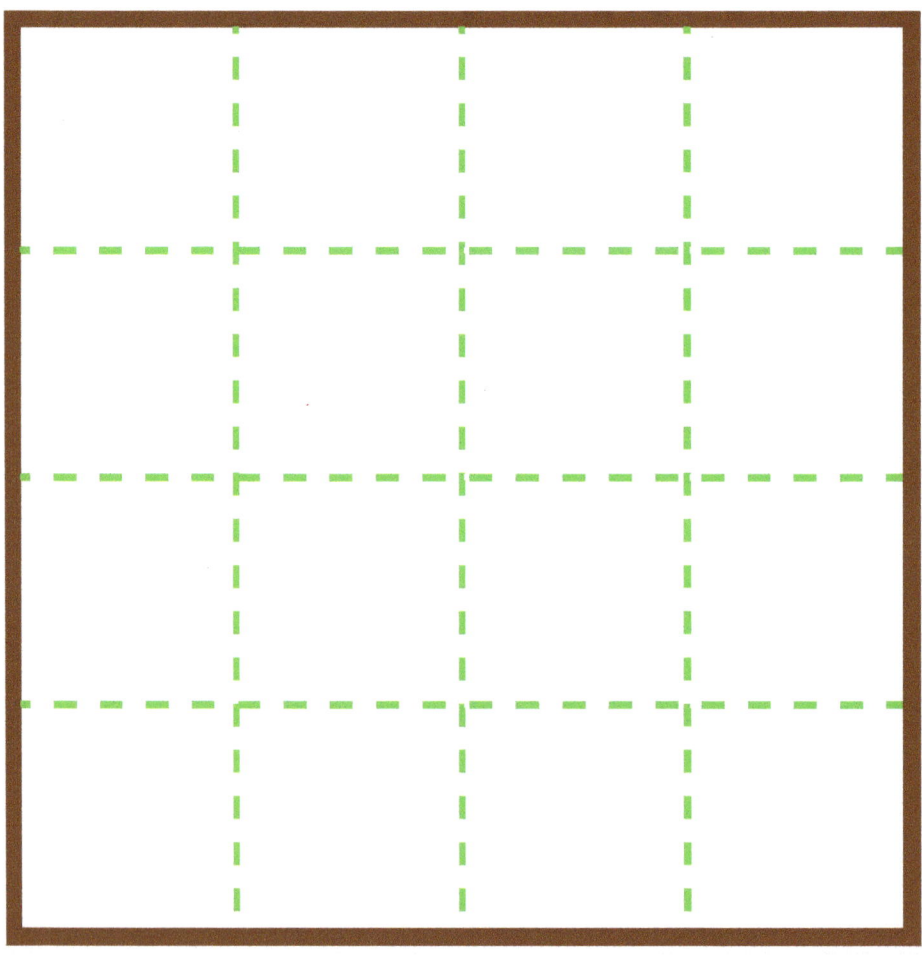

The Greenhorn Gardening Guide

Plan Out Your Garden

The Greenhorn Gardening Guide

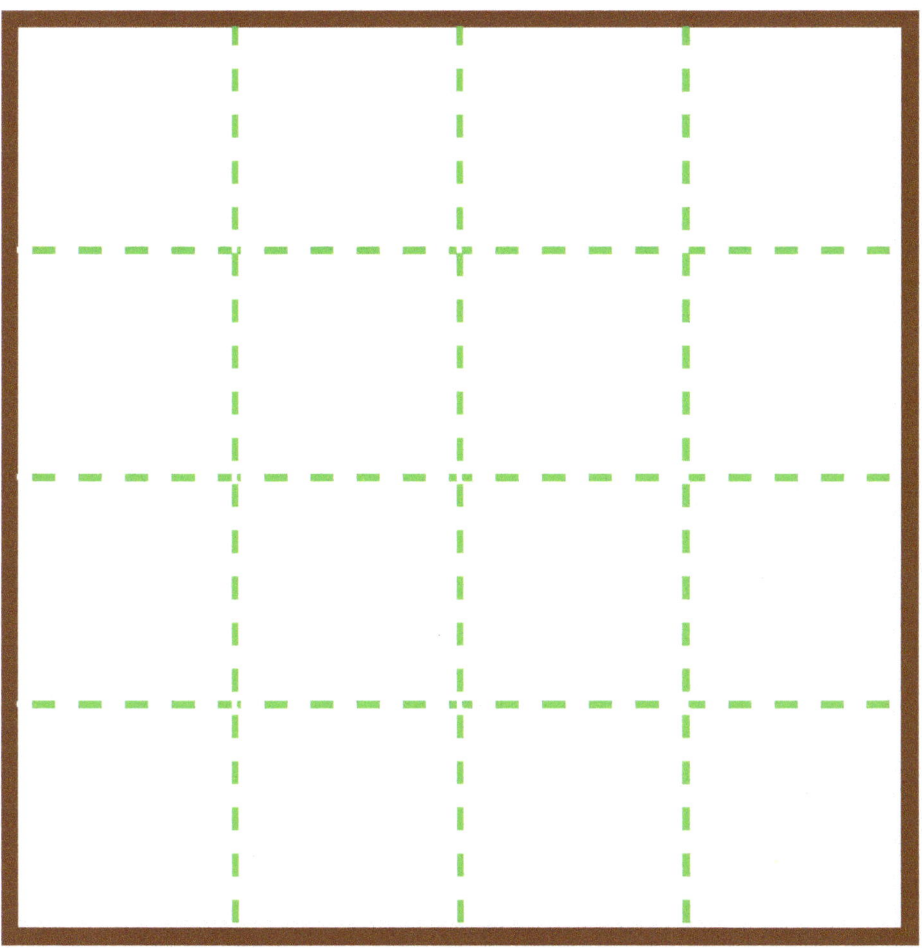

Plan Out Your Garden

Take Notes

It's important to document what you see and learn in your garden. Write down what you observe about your plants, soil, weather, bugs, successes, failures, and anything else you can think of! Not only will you enjoy looking back at your notes, but records of everything that did and didn't work for you is helpful when making future decisions for your garden.

Subject	Notes
Tomatoes	Cherry variety growing so fast!

The Greenhorn Gardening Guide

Plan Out Your Garden

The Greenhorn Gardening Guide

Need more space? Grab a nice notebook and keep going!

TEACH Services, Inc.
P U B L I S H I N G

We invite you to view the complete
selection of titles we publish at:
www.TEACHServices.com

We encourage you to write us
with your thoughts about this,
or any other book we publish at:
info@TEACHServices.com

TEACH Services' titles may be purchased in
bulk quantities for educational, fund-raising,
business, or promotional use.
bulksales@TEACHServices.com

Finally, if you are interested in seeing
your own book in print, please contact us at:
publishing@TEACHServices.com
We are happy to review your manuscript at no charge.

www.ingramcontent.com/pod-product-compliance
Lightning Source LLC
Chambersburg PA
CBHW060837170426
43192CB00019BA/2813